NOTE TO

Apologetics Press is a non-profit organization dedicated to the defense of New Testament Christianity. For over a quarter of a century, we have provided faith-building materials for adults. We also have produced numerous materials (like *Discovery* magazine, our *Explorer Series*, and various books) for young people in third grade through high school. We now are pleased to present a new series of books for even younger children.

The Apologetics Press Early Reader Series is a set of books aimed at children in kindergarten through second grade. Depending on the age of your children, this series is flexible enough to allow parents to read to their children, read along with their children, or they can listen while their children read aloud to them.

The books in this series are filled with beautiful full-color pictures and wonderful information about God, His creation, and His Word. These books are written on a level that early readers will enjoy, while drawing them closer to their Creator.

We hope you enjoy using the Apologetics Press Early Reader Series to encourage your children to read, while at the same time helping them learn about God and His creation.

God Made Animals

by Eric Lyons

Copyright © 2005
Apologetics Press

ISBN-10: 0-932859-70-4

ISBN-13: 978-0-932859-70-9

Library of Congress: 2005926996

Printed in China

God Made Animals

by
Eric Lyons

Animals and people have been living together on the Earth since day six of Creation.

Since the time of Adam and Eve,
men and women have studied
God's wonderful creatures.
We have learned a lot about them.

WELCOME TO
MAESA ELEPHANT CAMP

God made the elephant
with a big body and a
long trunk. Some elephants
grow to weigh more
than a school bus.

Cougars are big cats that live in the wild. They can jump up to 18 feet high. That is almost twice as high as a basketball goal.

God designed camels with humps on their backs. Some camels have only one hump. Others have two humps.

Camels store fat in their humps. When they have to go without food for a long time, their bodies use this fat for food. Camels have the ability to go a week (or more) without a drink of water.

The otter's webbed feet
and long tail make it a
great swimmer.

Flamingos are pink birds with long legs. You will often see these birds standing on one leg when they are eating and sleeping.

The cheetah is the fastest
land animal on Earth.
It is faster than some cars.

The ostrich is the biggest bird in the world. Unlike most birds, the ostrich cannot fly, but it can run really fast.

Penguins are another kind of
bird that cannot fly. Most penguins
live where it is very cold.

The sea horse has a head that looks like a horse's head. The sea horse changes colors when danger is near.

Turtles are some of the
slowest animals on Earth.
God designed them with
a hard shell that keeps
most other animals
from eating them.

One animal slower than the turtle is  the sloth. It takes a sloth a whole hour to travel the length of a football field.

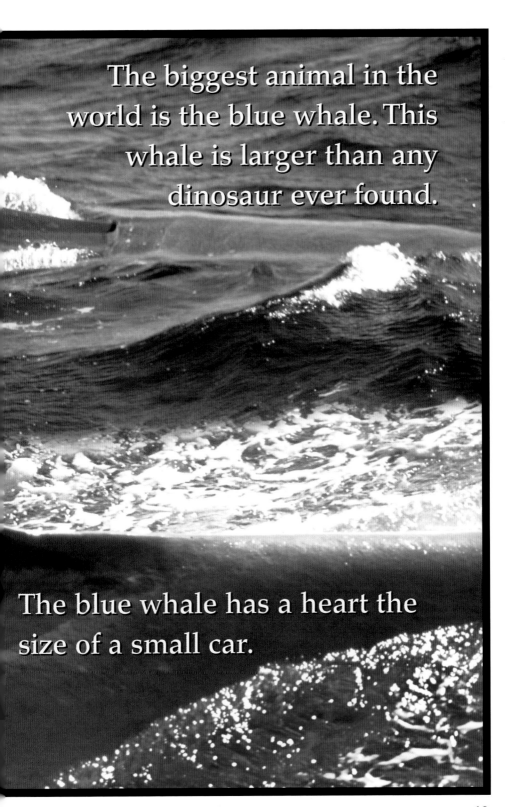

The biggest animal in the world is the blue whale. This whale is larger than any dinosaur ever found.

The blue whale has a heart the size of a small car.

Monkeys are fun to
watch at the zoo.
As you can see, God made
monkeys different from you.

God created
kangaroos
with special
pouches
where baby
kangaroos
live.

Baby kangaroos
are called
joeys.

The panda bear spends at least 12 hours each day eating bamboo. It eats more food in one day than what you eat in a whole week.

The lion is the "king of the jungle." Nothing seems to scare him.

The bill of a
platypus was
well designed
to gather food
from the bottom
of rivers.

Rattlesnakes use
their rattles to sound a
warning when they feel
danger is near.

Skunks are some of the
stinkiest animals in the world.
God gave them the ability
to spray a smelly liquid
from beneath their tail
when they get scared.

Most polar bears
live where
it is very
cold.

God made
these animals with
a good sense of smell.

God made many
different kinds of sharks.
Some are bigger than
a truck. Others are
small enough to fit
inside a toolbox.

Who made sharks to be
such good swimmers?

Giraffes are the tallest animals in the world. Their long necks help them find food that other animals cannot reach.

God
made the
woodpecker
with the ability
to peck a tree
trunk without
hurting its head.

God created all of these
wonderful animals.
Have you thanked
God today for His
wonderful creation?